The Holy Piby

The Blackman's Bible

Robert Athlyi Rogers

ISBN # 1453814760 and EAN-13 # 9781453814765

CONTENTS

PREFACE... 6
PROCLAMATION OF THE HOUSE OF ATHLYI... 8

THE FIRST BOOK OF ATHLYI CALLED ATHLYI
CHAPTER 1- THE CREATION... 9
CHAPTER 2- DEAD BECAME ALIVE... 10

THE SECOND BOOK OF ATHLYI CALLED AGGREGATION
CHAPTER 1- HEAVEN GRIEVED... 13
CHAPTER 2- PRESENTATION OF THE LAW... 21
CHAPTER 3- GOD'S HOLY LAW TO THE CHILDREN OF ETHIOPIA... 23
CHAPTER 4- THE LAW PREACHED... 28
CHAPTER 5- ATHLICANITY PREACHED... 30
CHAPTER 6- SOLEMNITY FEAST... 35
CHAPTER 7- MARCUS GARVEY... 43
CHAPTER 8- ATHLYI SENT ABROAD... 45
CHAPTER 9- THE WORD OF THE LORD... 47
CHAPTER 10- REJOICING IN THE LIGHT... 50
CHAPTER 11- RETURNED TO NEWARK... 52
CHAPTER 12- THE GUIDING LIGHT... 56
CHAPTER 13- ATHLYI BLEEDS... 58
CHAPTER 14- HEAVEN AND HELL... 61

CHAPTER 15- THE BEGGAR... 67

THE THIRD BOOK OF ATHLYI NAMED THE FACTS OF THE APOSTLES
CHAPTER 1- APOSTLES ANOINTED... 72
CHAPTER 2- GOD SPOKE TO HIS APOSTLES... 74
CHAPTER 3- STANDING BEFORE ELIJAH... 76
CHAPTER 4- APOSTLES EXALTED... 77

THE FOURTH BOOK OF ATHLYI CALLED PRECAUTION
CHAPTER I- A BUGGY FROM TOKIO TO LOS ANGELES... 79
CHAPTER 2- HELD OUT HIS MORSEL... 83
CHAPTER 3- THE CLEAN SHOULD NOT ACCEPT THE INVITATIONS OF THE UNCLEAN... 85
CHAPTER 4- SHALL SUFFER... 87

QUESTIONS AND ANSWERS... 90

THE SHEPHERD'S COMMAND BY ATHLYI... 93

PREFACE

The Holy Piby, a book founded by the Holy Spirit to deliver the gospel commanded by the Almighty God for the full salvation of Ethiopia's posterities.

In time the *Piby* shall contain all worthy prophecies and inspirations endowed by God upon the sons and daughters of Ethiopia, but no article shall be permitted to enter the *Piby* save that which is in accordance with the gospel of the twentieth century, preached by his Holiness, Shepherd Athlyi, apostle Marcus Garvey and colleague; the three apostles anointed and sent forth by the Almighty God to lay the foundation of industry, liberty and justice unto the generations of Ethiopia that they prove themselves a power among the nations and in the glory of their God.

The *Piby* is strictly Holy, dedicated to the cause of saving souls for God upon which the Afro Athlican Constructive Church is built, therefore articles not agreeable shall not be entered upon or under the covers thereof.

Help to build Athlican Colleges, prepare your sons and daughters for a high position in the Athlican organization.

For deep, energy shifting Chakra healing programs on CD, MP3, MP4 and DVD, plus free downloads:

www.ChakraHealingSounds.com

PROCLAMATION OF THE HOUSE OF ATHLYI

Woodbridge, N.J., U.S.A. March 1924

His Holiness, Shepherd Athlyi, 1st of the House of Athlyi, supreme lord of the Afro Athlican Constructive Church, requests that all Negroes the world over celebrate concord in its fullness.

The first of August all members of the A.A.C. Church shall join in with the Universal Negro Improvement Association that there be a united day of joviality.

O God, bless thine Apostles, and help us to establish a Heaven on earth.

Proclamated by the
HOUSE OF ATHLYI

THE FIRST BOOK OF ATHLYI CALLED ATHLYI

CHAPTER I

THE CREATION

From the beginning there was God and he spake and all things were made that are made.

The sixth day God made man for his glory, and all things were given unto him for his possession and for his use the woman hath God made of man and for the glory of the man that she serve him and raise up seed unto him.

And God rested the seventh day and hallowed it that men should do also.

Now when the man saw the woman that was made of him and for his glory, he loved her and married with her, consequently she bore children unto Him and they became the father and mother of all men.

And God called the man Adam and the woman Eve. They were of a mixed complexion.

And it came to pass that God commanded the man to give names to all things that are made.

CHAPTER 2

DEAD BECAME ALIVE

And it came to pass that God entered the body of an unknown dead and the dead became alive, then did he walk about the earth in person. He dwelt among men and wrought many miracles so that the Kingdom of heaven might be verified. He suffered persecution and privation as an example of what ministers of the gospel must suffer to maintain the kingdom of God among men.

And it came to pass that God gave his name Elijah, and he called upon the name of the Lord God even though he himself was God.

Now when the time had appeared for God to return, the supreme angel commanded the chariot of heaven to meet him. And when the chariot appeared unto Elijah, he ascended and returned to his throne in heaven where he reigned from the beginning and shall, unto the end, King of kings, and God of gods.

Had the men in the days of Elijah's visit on earth taken a right record of his administration, long before this day the inhabitants of this earth would have known him as God of all men.

For in Elijah do the heavenly host worship as God of the universe and in him do I, Athlyi, believe as the only God.

He is the Lord of righteousness and of love, an industrious God, brave, omnipotent, omnipresent, a king of sympathy and of justice, giver of power and salvation, upon this God, and him only, his law and the Holy Ghost shall the Athlyians build their church.

We shall endeavour to please and serve him, for he is our God. We shall worship him with all our hearts and with all our souls, for unto us there is none so good as the Lord, our God. When the Lord God of Ethiopia is with us in the battle for that to which we are entitled, show me the foe so powerful to set us down? Verily I say unto you there is none.

But who can be so good as to please the conscience of the people that they say ye are of God? Who will pay such a price? Will you? Then, if so, lay down and let the public trod upon your head for a good name.

Verily I say unto you for this the Athlyians are bad, but on the scale of Justice, let them not be found wanting. Then shall they please the Lord God, maker of heaven and earth, and great shall be their reward in the kingdom of heaven.

For deep, energy shifting Chakra healing programs on CD, MP3, MP4 and DVD, plus free downloads:

www.ChakraHealingSounds.com

THE SECOND BOOK OF ATHLYI CALLED AGGREGATION

CHAPTER 1

HEAVEN GRIEVED

For as much as the children of Ethiopia, God's favorite people of old, have turned away from his divine Majesty, neglecting life economic, believing they could on spiritual wings fly to the kingdom of God, consequently became a dependent for the welfare of others.

Therefore the whole heaven was grieved and there was a great lamentation in the Kingdom of God. Ethiopian mothers whose bodies have been dead for a thousand years, weeping for their suffering generations and shall not be comforted.

And behold two angels of the Lord resembling two saints of Ethiopia appeared before Athlyi and he inquired of them what is the cry?

And they answered him saying, Ethiopian mothers who have been dead a thousand years pleading before Elijah for the redemption of suffering Ethiopia and her posterities who by the feet of the nations are trodden.

Convention in Heaven

There is a great convention in heaven, saith the angels of the Lord, unto you this day we are sent by the Lord to felicitate. For thou art appointed the shepherd to lead Ethiopia's generations from the oppressive feet of the nations, and there are appointed also prophets to prepare the way before thee.

And it came to pass when Athlyi heard these sayings he feared with great astonishment and turned his face from the angels of the Lord. And there appeared unto him his divine highness Jesus Christ, Prince of the Kingdom of God, and said quickly behold the messengers of my Father.

At this saying Athlyi turned again to the angels of the Lord and said, thy will be done, O God of Ethiopia, but how can I be the shepherd, to lead millions of millions even from the end of the earth when as I am but a twig before the eyes of men?

The Heavens Open

And the angels of the Lord answered him saying, a twig that is made by the Holy Spirit, an instrument to lead men, is great in the sight of p 27 God, over which the armies of the earth or the hosts of hell shall not prevail.

And it came to pass that the angel who had the less to say lifted her eyes to heaven and stretched forth her arms over the earth and cried, blessed be thou Ethiopia, glory be the Father, thou Elijah, Hosanna, Hosanna to Jehovah, praise ye Douglas the convention have triumph.

There appeared a beautiful light on earth and when the light flashed Athlyi looked toward the heaven, and behold the heaven was -open and there was a great host of saints robed in blue, millions of millions as far as his eyes could see there was a mighty host.

When Athlyi sought the angels of the Lord they were

not and he heard a voice say "Athlyi" and another "Athlyi" and he looked up and saw two angels ascending towards the celestial host.

Ethiopia Anointed

And when the two messengers of the Lord were midways they cried out unto the earth saying, blessed be thou Ethiopia for this day thou art anointed, thou are blest with a blessing, be ye forever united and stand up, let the world know your God.

And when the two angels of the Lord neared the multitude the whole host roared with a thunder of joy that shook the earth like a mighty earthquake.

And it came to pass that an angel robed in four colours came forward to receive them and the whole celestial multitude stood and quietly formed an aisle.

And when the two messengers appeared before the heavenly host they bowed to the multitude and turned themselves around and bowed also to the earth.

Then came forward the mighty Angel robed in four

colors and placed a gold ring upon their heads, and came forward also two mothers of Ethiopia, each with a star in their right hand, and pinned them on the left breast of the two messengers of the Lord.

And it came to pass that heaven and earth shook three times and the two angels marched up the aisle and joined with the multitude.

Rejoicing in Heaven

There was great rejoicing in Heaven and singing hosanna to Elijah; praise ye Douglas; blessed be thou Ethiopia forever and forever; the people at the end of the known world, and world p. 29 unknown, shall look for the coming of thy children with food and with rainment.

And when the two angels had joined the multitude and the mighty angel had finished his performance the said angel who was robed in colors turned to the heavenly host and said:

"Mothers of Ethiopia, the convention has triumphed, your sorrows have brought joy to Ethiopia, your tears have anointed her soil with a blessing, your cries have awakened her children throughout the earth, yea in the corners of the unknown world are they aroused, and is prophesying, saying prepare ye the way for a redeemer."

Shepherd Anointed

For unto Ethiopia this day a Shepherd is anointed, yea, as a shepherd gathers his sheep so shall he gather unto God, the generation of Ethiopia even from the end of the earth and lead them high, a nation among nations.

Then shall the inhabitants of the earth know that the Lord our God has not forsaken Ethiopia, and that the mighty is weak against his command, and unto no nation has he given power forever.

Verily I say unto you, woe be unto the persecutors of the shepherd for he is anointed by the Lord our God, therefore one drop of his blood or the least of his apostles whom he has anointed to administer the law to the generations of Ethiopia, or the blood of a prophet within the law, shall break to pieces the oppressors of Ethiopia.

The Mighty Angel

When the mighty angel had finished speaking to the heavenly host he then turned to the earth and said: "Children of Ethiopia, stand," and there flashed upon the earth a great multitude of Negroes knowing not from whence they came; then shouted instantly the whole heavenly host, "Behold, behold Ethiopia has triumphed."

And it came to pass that the mighty angel spoke to the multitude of Negroes, saying, "Woe be unto those who say to the shepherd, thou fool, or to the least of an apostle anointed to administer the law, for it is not the desire of the shepherd but the will of the Lord who is God."

Dominion Over the Shepherd

"For as much as the Lord has dominion over the shepherd and the shepherd over his apostles and the apostles over all the generations of Ethiopia; then shall the Lord our God administer to the shepherd and the shepherd to his apostles and the apostles to all the children of Ethiopia.

"Woe be unto an apostle who is anointed to administer the law and neglect or deny it. Verily he shall be cast out and the hand of the Lord shall come upon him with sorrow and disgrace.

"Woe be unto those who saith I will not be united, neither will I follow the shepherd, they shall be as sheep without a shepherd only to be destroyed by the wolf of the field.

"Woe be unto those who saith I hearken not to the voice of the shepherd but go the way of the majority, for in the majority the spirit of the lord will not be found.

"Woe be unto those who saith I will not worship in the house of the Lord subsidiary to the house of Athlyi."

Purification

"For as much as the house of Athlyi is founded by the holy spirit to purify the children of Ethiopia and to administer the holy law commanded to them by the Lord God of all mercies, that they in the end shall be ushered in the kingdom of his Divine Majesty by faith through consecration in love, justice and by the pledging of life's loyalty to a prolific and defensive cause for the welfare of mankind.

"Let not the least or the greatest of the children give a deaf ear to the saying of the shepherd thereof, for through the mouth of the shepherd cometh the word of the Lord to the adherents of the Holy Law."

CHAPTER 2

PRESENTATION OF THE LAW

And it came to pass that the mighty angel robed in four colors descended from among the great heavenly host.

When the Athlyi saw the angel descending he feared with great fear and hid behind the root of a tree.

But the angel of the Lord came upon him and said., "Athlyi, come forth for the Lord has made thee shepherd of his anointed children of Ethiopia. "

And Athlyi answered saying, "Who are thou?" "I am

Douglas, a messenger from the Lord," replied the angel. "I am sent to robe thee and to give in thy hands and in thy care the Lord's articles."

Verily no man shall take away that which the Lord giveth, for the word of the Lord who is God, will not come unto any save he who is appointed by the Father.

Athlyi Robed

The angel of the Lord robed Athlyi in four colors and commanded him to put forth his right hand and the messenger presented in his right hand a staff and in his left hand the Holy Law saying, "Go and administer this Law through thine apostles unto the children of Ethiopia and command them to rise from the feet of their oppressors. Great is the penalty if there be any failure on your part to deliver the Law; the hand of the Lord shall come upon thee with horror and thou shalt regret the day ye was born."

The angel of the Lord hesitated, then said to Athlyi "Swear before the Lord God that thou wilt administer the Law unto the children"; then Athlyi lifted his eyes to the heaven and said, "Heaven and earth bear witness to my saying, I will."

Then the messenger of the Lord touched Athlyi on his left breast with the first finger of his right hand saying, "Be thou brave," then disappeared from the presence of the shepherd.

CHAPTER 3

GOD'S HOLY LAW TO THE CHILDREN OF ETHIOPIA

Great and manifold are the blessings bestowed upon us the oppressed children of Ethiopia, by His Divine Majesty, Lord God Almighty, King of all mercies, when by his most holy command His divine highness, Christ, Prince of the Heavenly Kingdom, descended and anointed us that we may be prepared to receive these noble men, servants of God and redeemers of Ethiopia's posterities. His honor, Marcus Garvey and colleague, his holiness the shepherd Athlyi, supreme minister of God's Holy Law to the children of

Ethiopia, may we show gratitude to our God by being submissive to his teachings through these his humble servants, and submitting ourselves in obedience to his Holy Law that we a suffering people may reap the fruit thereof.

When as it was the intention of others to keep us forever in darkness, by our faithfulness to the Law we shall in time prove to the nations that God has not forsaken Ethiopia.

The Holy Commandments

I

Love ye one another, O children of Ethiopia, for by no other way can ye love the Lord your God.

II

Be thou industrious, thrifty and fruitful, O offsprings of Ethiopia, for by no other way can ye show gratitude to the Lord your God, for the many blessings he has bestowed upon earth free to all mankind.

III

Be ye concretized and ever united, for by the power of unity ye shall demand respect of the nations.

IV

Work ye willingly with all thy heart with all thy soul and with all thy strength to relieve suffering and oppressed humanity, for by no other way can ye render integral service to the Lord your God.

V

Be thou clean and pleasant, O generation of Ethiopia, for thou art anointed, moreover the angels of the Lord dwelleth with thee.

VI

Be thou punctual, honest and truthful that ye gain flavor in the sight of the Lord your God, and that your pathway be prosperous.

VII

Let no people take away that which the Lord thy God giveth thee, for the Lord shall inquire of it and if ye shall say some one hath taken it, ye shall in no wise escape punishment, for he that dieth in retreat of his enemy the Lord shall not hold him guiltless, but a people who dieth in pursuit of their enemy for the protection of that which the Lord God giveth them, shall receive a reward in the kingdom of their Father.

VIII

Thou shalt first bind up the wound of thy brother and correct the mistakes in thine own household before ye can see the sore on the body of your friend, or the error in the household of thy neighbour.

IX

O generation of Ethiopia, shed not the blood of thine own for the welfare of others for such is the pathway to destruction and contempt.

X

Be ye not contented in the vineyard or household of others, for ye know not the day or the hour when denial shall appear, prepare ye rather for yourselves a foundation, for by no other way can man manifest love for the offsprings of the womb.

XI

Athlyi, Athlyi, thou shepherd of the holy law and of the children of Ethiopia, establish ye upon the Law a Holy temple for the Lord according to thy name and there shall all the children of Ethiopia worship the Lord their God, and there shall the apostles of the shepherd administer the law and receive pledges thereto and concretize within the Law. Verily he that is concretized within the Law shall be a follower and a defender thereof, more-over the generations born of him that is concretize within the law are also of the law.

XII

O generation of Ethiopia, thou shalt have no other God but the Creator of Heaven and Earth and the things thereof. Sing ye praises and shout Hosanna to the Lord your God, while for a foundation ye sacrifice on earth for His Divine Majesty the Lord our Lord in six days created. the heaven and earth and rested the seventh; ye also shall hallow the seventh day, for it is blessed by the Lord, therefore on this day thou shall do no manner of work or any within thy gates.

The Shepherd's Prayer By Athlyi

O God of Ethiopia, thy divine majesty; thy spirit come in our hearts to dwell in the path of righteousness, lead us, help us to forgive that we may be forgiven, teach us love and loyalty on earth as in Heaven, endow us with wisdom and understanding to do thy will, thy blessing to us that the hungry be fed, the naked clothed, the sick nourished, the aged protected and the infants cared for. Deliver us from the hands of our enemies that we prove fruitful, then in the last day when life is o'er, our bodies in the clay, or in the depths of the sea, or in the belly of a beast, O give our souls a place in thy kingdom forever and forever. Amen.

CHAPTER 4

THE LAW PREACHED

Now in the year of 1917 A.D., Shepherd Athlyi first went about the City of Newark, New Jersey, U.S.A., telling of the Law and preaching concretation saying, I come not only to baptize but to concretize for the rescue of suffering humanity, for verily I say unto you, first seek ye righteousness toward men and all things will be added unto you, even the kingdom of God.

There came to him many to be concretized and he concretized them with water, men and women. And the names of his stars were: Rev. J.H. Harris, Sister R.J. Hamilton, Brother J. Reid, Rev. and Mrs. J. Barber, Brother C.C. Harris, Sister Leila Best, Sister Thurston, Brother H. Pope, Rev. and Mrs. Flanagan, Brother Charles McLaurin, Sister Letica Johnson, Brother and Sister Adam Costly, Brother and Sister W.D. Sullivan, Sister Sarah Johnson, Brother G.W. Roberts, Rev. J.J. Derricks, Rev. A.J. Green, Rev. W. Barclift, Sister Bertha Johnson, Her holiness, the Shepherdess Miriam, Her Holiness the Shepherdmiss Muriel, Brother F.L. Redd. These are those who followed the shepherd from place to place.

And it came to pass that his holiness, the shepherd, traveled to Springfield, Massachusetts, U.S.A., there he concretized with water, and the names of his stars who followed him around were: Sister Sylvie Randall, Brother and Sister Eugene Kitchen, Brother and Sister

Joseph Rutherford, Rev. R.G. Gaines, Brother J. When, Sister Ellen Frazier, Sister Minnieolo Walker, Sister M.A. Bryant, Irene Chambers, E. Dempsey. From there he traveled all around South America and the West Indies, preaching of the law and concretation by water for the sake of suffering humanity.

Moreover, in the year of 1919 Athlyi, after he was anointed shepherd, paraded the streets of Newark with a host of Negroes, protected by riding officers of the city and accompanied by a Salvation Army carrying banners, proclaiming a universal holiday for Negroes and foretelling of their industrial and national independence.

CHAPTER 5

ATHLICANITY PREACHED

For as much as the doctrine preached by Athlyi gained favor in the hearts of the people, and that it was efficient for the Salvation of Ethiopia's generations: On the thirteenth day of the seventh month, in the nineteen hundred and eighteenth year, the followers of Athlyi assembled at the Israel Memorial A.M.E. Church, West Kinney Street, Newark, New Jersey, U.S.A. They declared themselves Athlyians by name and in faith.

And they consolidated themselves within the faith. They sang songs of praises and offered thanksgiving to the Lord God of Ethiopia.

And it came to pass that a committee was appointed from among them to confirm the Shepherd, and the names of those appointed and consolidated were Sister Rachel Hamilton, Rev. James Barber, Sister Gilby Rose, Bro. C.E. Harris and Bro. James Reed.

The committee decorated the Shepherd in four colors and committed in his right hand a staff so as to confirm the authority conferred upon him by the heavenly officials.

Now when the Shepherd was adorned and anointed by prayer, the Athlyians shouted with great joy and cried "Lead on, Shepherd of the Athlyians."

And it came to pass after the performance, the Shepherd stood up, and he was in four colors which were blue, black, red and green, and he explained the meaning of the colors and of the staff.

Saying Ethiopia's generations shall respect the heaven while for a foundation they sacrifice on earth; moreover a king sits on the throne of his organized government, but a Shepherd must seek his sheep and prepare a pasture for them that they be fed.

Then the Shepherd commanded his followers to stand, and he taught them saying, great is His Divine Majesty, the Lord God of all mankind, Father of Ethiopia; Who is greater than the Lord God? Even from the beginning of the world hath he prepared for his children unto the end.

The sun, the moon, the stars, the wind, the rain, the land and the sea hath he given free to mankind; who is so philanthropic, so magnificent, who can give such a gift? There is none so great as the Lord our God.

Let all the generations of Ethiopia hear the voice of Athlyi, for in his hands the law is given unto them.

Let not be devil persuade you that you turn your back against the Lord God of Ethiopia.

Woe be unto you should the heavenly father because of your ingratitudes turn against thee, revengely the hands of thy enemies and shall come upon thee with horror.

Let the Athlyians walk in the path of righteousness and all impediments shall be their foot stool and the spirit of the Lord shall dwell with them for ever and ever.

Blessed are the industrious hearts for they are those who use the blessing and the power of God for the good of mankind. Great shall be their reward in the kingdom of heaven.

Blessed are those who seek the Lord and by actual work prove to the nations that they have found him; for the power of God shall be as two kings feeling in darkness for an electric switch and he that found it immediately there was light throughout his palace and all the people rejoiced because of its splendor, but in the palace of him that found it not, there was no light, therefore his people wandered and became the servants of others.

Blessed are a people who seek their own, beautify and

maintain it, for in their barns there shall be plenty; great shall they be among men. The Lord shall glory in them and their daughters shall be the wives of mighty men.

Woe be unto a people, a race who seek not their own foundation; their wives shall be servants for the wives of other men, and their daughters shall be wives of poor men and of vagabonds, and there shall be tears because of privation, then in the end hell everlasting for there shall be no reward in the kingdom of heaven for slothful nor the unconcerned.

Woe be unto a race of people who forsake their own and adhere to the doctrine of another. They shall be slaves to the people thereof.

Verily I say unto you, O children of Ethiopia, boast not of the progress of other races, believing that thou are a part of the project for at any time thou shall be cast over the bridge of death both body and soul.

Forget not the assembling of thy selves and unitedly working for the up building of Ethiopia and her generations.

Then shall the nations of the earth respect thee and

thy commodities shall be for their gold and their commodities for thy gold, but there shall be none to fool thee neither shall ye be their slaves.

For thy emblem shall rank among their emblems; thy ships among their ships, and thy men-of-war among their men-of-war; great shall be thy name among the nations.

The Lord God, Father of Ethiopia, shall glory in thee, with thee shall all the angels rejoice, great is thy reward in the kingdom of heaven.

Thy daughters shall work with clean hands and in soft clothing, thy sons shall enjoy the fruits of their colleges.

CHAPTER 6

SOLEMNITY FEAST

The following meeting after the Shepherd was confirmed, there came to him men and women to be concretized, and he concretized them with water.

And the Shepherd taught the form Solemnity feast,

which the Christians call sacrament, and he taught the form of baptism also concretation and the period of concord according to the Athlican faith.

Let the people be baptized with water by submersion for the remission of their iniquities in the name of one God, his Holy Law and the Holy Ghost.

Let the people be concretized also with water that they be binded into one united band from one generation to another and let them pledge their lives loyally to the cause of actual work for the up building of Ethiopia and for the rescue of suffering humanity, suffer them to wash their hands against the slothful and fruitless life of the past. Then shall the parson give to them a hand of fellowship, bringing them forward into a new and ever productive life.

Let the people assemble once a month on their knees before the altar at Solemnity feast, then shall the parson and ordained cleffs administer to them bread and water, saying "eat in remembrance of your pledge to God, yielding yourselves into actual work for the welfare of your generation through the up building of Ethiopia and for the rescue of suffering humanity.

Drink in remembrance of your baptism when thy sins hath been washed away, bid far the devil and his iniquities; arise and go in the name of one God, His Law and the Holy Ghost.

For as much as angel Douglas binded the heaven and earth for the rescue of Ethiopia and her posterities, suffer the children of Ethiopia to assemble for three days celebration, beginning from the setting of the sun on the twenty-ninth day of the seventh month unto the setting of the sun of the first day of the eighth month of the year, which shall be known throughout the world as the period of concord in accordance with the celestial and terrestrial concord led by the mighty angel Douglas.

Hear, oh generations of Ethiopia, for I, Athlyi, speak not as a mere man but with authority from the kingdom of God.

Verily, I say unto you, the first days of the concord thou shall not eat the flesh of any animals, nor large fishes, neither shall ye drink of their blood or of their milk, thy victuals shall be of fowl and tiny fishes, devote thyself in communing with the Lord God of Ethiopia.

Be aware of improper conduct, for the angels of heaven are participating in the concord.

On the third day, which is the last day of concord, let there be a great feast and joviality among the people.

Let the atmosphere be teemed with balloons of colors carried in the hands of the people; let also the possessions of all Ethiopia's generations be adorned with the colors.

During the concord the house of Athlyi shall order the release of the people from all Athlican factories, or other enterprises so that they can commune with the Lord their God.

In time of concord let the Athlican ships fly the colors of the Great Negro Civilization where so ever they are; pray that the captains thereof are of the Athlican faith so as to celebrate concord in its fullness.

Hear ye, O generations of Ethiopia, for I, Athlyi, speak unto you, for as the Lord God of Ethiopia liveth, this is a serious affair which must not be forsaken.

The Holy finger print of the Almighty God signed the issue in the name of His Majesty, His Law, and for the sake of suffering humanity.

And it came to pass that one of the newcomers into the Athlican Faith who sat in the midst of the audience spoke, saying, "May I ask his Holiness, what is the principal belief of the Athlyians?"

Straight-way the Shepherd answered saying, the fundamental belief of the Athlican faith is justice to all, but hear ye, also, the Athlyian's creed:

The Athlyian's Creed

We believe in one God, maker of all things, Father of Ethiopia and then in His Holy Law as it is written in the book Piby, the sincerity of Angel Douglas and the power of the Holy Ghost. We believe in one Shepherd Athlyi as an anointed apostle of the Lord our God, then in the Afro Athlican Constructive Church unto the most Holy House of Athlyi. We believe in the Freedom of Ethiopia and the maintenance of an efficient government recorded upon the catalog of nations in honor of her posterities and the glory of her God, the establishment of true love and the administration of Justice to all men, the celebration of concord, the virtue of the Solemnity feast and in the form of baptism and concretation as taught by our Shepherd Athlyi.

We believe in the utilization of the power and blessings of God for the good of mankind, the creation of industries, the maintenance of colleges and the unity of force, then in the end when earth toil is over we shall be rewarded a place of rest in the kingdom of Heaven, thereto sing with the saints of Ethiopia, singing Hallelujah, hosanna to the Lord our God forever and ever Amen.

Then the Athlyians shouted "Hosanna to the Lord God, surely the Lord has sent us not only a Shepherd but a savior."

Straight-way the Shepherd Athlyi spake, saying "Upon those words the Afro Athlican Constructive Church stands firm over which the hosts of hell nor the armies of the earth shall not prevail."

And the Shepherd being full with the Holy Spirit

recited from his heart saying: "Father, thou God of all, closer to thee even though afar we stray; thou hast called us back, now all in one we come, children in Africa: Closer, oh God, to thee; closer to thee."

And he began to tell his followers about the wonderful works of God; how he hath sent apostles of the twentieth century, to save Ethiopia and her generations from the oppressive feet of the nations that they prove themselves fruitful for the good of their children and the glory of their God.

"Know ye that I am not the only one sent by the Lord our God to rescue the children of Ethiopia, for before me there were two others sent forth to prepare the minds of the people for the great things that shall come to pass.

"I saw an angel resembling a mighty Negro, and upon his head were horns of a great structure and on his breast was a map of life.

"I heard a great voice uttered from the end of the world saying, behold the map of the new Negroes, by this shall ye know the apostle of the twentieth century whom the Almighty God hath commanded to save

Ethiopia and her posterities.

"At the sound of the mighty voice the structure descended from the head of the angel and stood upon the ground and the map surrounded it, then was the writing plain to be understood."

And the Shepherd showed the people a copy of the map, and said "Behold the map as I have seen it, straight-way at midnight I reproduce the mystery."

Then the Athlyians shouted for joy and the Shepherd spake with a loud voice saying "Thou sun that shines upon the waters of the utmost world, that gives light to the earth, stand thou still over mountains of Africa and give light to her righteous armies."

Where are those? There is none to compare with the Athlyians in united spirits and a determination; a people, lovers of freedom and of justice, fearless of death.

CHAPTER 7

MARCUS GARVEY

Now in the year of nineteen hundred and nineteen on the thirtieth day of the seventh month, when the Athlyians were celebrating concord in the City of Newark, New Jersey, U.S.A., and on the third day of the period a paper was read by the Rev. Bonfield telling of Marcus Garvey in New York City.

And the Shepherd hesitated, then spake, saying: "I almost believe this is one of the apostles of the twentieth century, but where is the other? For I look for two, however by the map of life I shall know him.

"Raise not the weight of your finger on Marcus Garvey, neither speak ye against him."

In the year of 1921 Garvey spake saying: "I have no time to teach religion."

Because of this saying Athlyi took up his pen and was about to declare him not an apostle of the twentieth century.

And it came to pass that the word of the Lord came to Athlyi saying, "Blame not this man for I the Lord God hath sent him to prepare the minds of Ethiopia's generations, verily he shall straighten up upon the map."

Nevertheless in the year nineteen hundred and twenty two, Apostle Garvey issued a religious call throughout the world which fulfilled the last item upon the map of life.

Therefore, Athlyi yielded him a copy of the map, and declared Marcus Garvey an apostle of the Lord God for the redemption of Ethiopia and her suffering posterities.

And the word of the Lord came to Athlyi saying, "I am the Lord God of Ethiopia, three apostles of the twentieth century have I sent forth unto Ethiopia's generations to administer the Law and the Gospel which I have commanded for their salvation, let not the hands of men ordain them. For I, the Lord, hath anointed mine apostles that they may ordain and give authority to ordain."

CHAPTER 8

ATHLYI SENT ABROAD

And it came to pass that the word of the Lord came to Athlyi saying, "Get thee into foreign countries and provide stars of the Law and of the gospel of the twentieth century."

"Go the way of the Atlantic and return by way of the Pacific," and Athlyi obeyed the Lord.

And when he was in the Strait of Magellan, the Lord spake to him saying.

"My holy house of Athlyi let her be of two wings, the Church to the right and a green pasture to the left.

"Let the Church teach and the green pasture to provide for the people; let the house of Athlyi be the director thereof, and I, the Lord, shall dwell in the house of Athlyi and give light to her wings, then shall the inhabitants of the earth know that I am the Lord God of Ethiopia.

"Let there be but one church of denomination upon

the Law and the gospel commanded for the salvation of Ethiopia's generations.

"In entering the inner door of the Church let the people bow with reverence to the holy dictuary."

Suffer no one to preach upon or in the dictuary save a teacher of the Law and a believer in the gospel commanded to the children of Ethiopia.

Let the people take interest in the apostles, but he that boost not the green pasture to provide for the people is not worthy of compensation.

Let the people give to the green pasture for their own good and for the welfare of their generations.

Oh Athlyians, love ye one another, forget not the assembling of yourselves together that no corruption gather between thee, for thou art the light and guide unto salvation; Let all the children of Ethiopia follow thee.

May the Lord God of Ethiopia watch between us whilst we are absent one from another. May he endow us with unity of spirit and anxious hearts to again assemble for the rise of falling humanity through the guidance of the house of Athlyi and in the name of one God, his Law and the Holy Ghost for ever and ever. Amen.

CHAPTER 9

THE WORD OF THE LORD

And it came to pass in the year of nineteen hundred and twenty four and the twelfth day of the ninth month, the word of the Lord, God of Ethiopia came to Athlyi saying:

"I am God, the Creator, Father of Ham, Canaan, Nimrod and Ethiopia."

"Why calleth thou my Holy Temple, Church?" sayeth the Lord unto Athlyi.

"Will thou also destroy the righteousness of my holy name?"

"Will thou even so teach that I am a God who confers honor upon the envious in mind, the lying, inhuman, murdering, plunderous, oppressive and adulterous characters in my name?"

And the Lord continued to say, "Athlyi! Oh Athlyi! I say unto you again. Why calleth my holy temple, 'Church'? Will thou also teach that I have commanded to destroy the offsprings of Ham in Canaan?"

Athlyi answered saying, "Father, behold the house of Athlyi."

"This I have created," saith the Lord, "Verily I shall dwell in the High place at the House of Athlyi and shall give light to the Shepherd and the Shepherd to his Apostles and his Apostles to all people who shall constitute the auxiliaries of my most Holy house of Athlyi.

"But why calleth thou these auxiliaries, 'Church'?" he continued.

Athlyi hesitated and the Lord our God, who stood in the midst of a brilliant light, like unto a circle pointed to Athlyi and said: "I have commanded thee but thou art carried away by those who polluted the righteousness of my name."

At this saying Athlyi advanced towards the Lord with open arms and cried out, "O God of Ethiopia, I pray, redeem me, wash me clean and separate me from all gospels that pollute the righteousness of thy name that those in me unto thee may be clean and free from all things abominable in thy sight."

"Thou art the supreme sage; pray! give me to nurse at thy breast the milk of wisdom that I may know and understand thee."

And it came to pass that the Lord, our God of Ethiopia, spoke saying, "Reach out and touch me."

Athlyi reached out and with the first finger of his right hand touched the personality in the light, straightway his heart became in motion and the eyes of Athlyi lit up like a torch. Evidently he had increased in wisdom, a man matchless in spirit.

And the Lord, God of Ethiopia, spoke unto Athlyi saying, "Thou art a star in my crown. Go ye through the lands that men may dwell in thee and see clear the impediments in the paths of their lives."

Now when the Lord had commanded Athlyi to carry the light unto others he departed and the light of his eyes lit up the near and distant darkness, and the word of his mouth brought freedom to the enslaved.

Footnotes

58:3 Cf. Gen. 10:6-7: "By these were the borders of the nations divided in their lands; every one after his tongue, after their families, in their nations. And the sons of Ham: Cush, and Mizraim, and Put, and Canaan."

59:4 Gen. 10:24-27: "And Noah awoke from his wine, and knew what his younger son [Ham] had done unto him. And he said, Cursed be Canaan; a servant of servants shall he be unto his brethren."

CHAPTER 10

REJOICING IN THE LIGHT

And it came to pass on the following day the Lord called Athlyi; and when Athlyi appeared before the Lord, the light of his eyes connected with the light that surrounded the Divine Personality.

And there appeared a light matchless in its beauty. Straightway the whole celestial host shouted and there appeared millions of Angels dancing in the light singing, "Behold! Behold Ethiopia! the bride of the master. Her day has come at last! The Lord has received her hand. Her night has forever passed."

The Lord stretched forth his hands over the earth and there appeared millions of black men, women and children, who joined with the angels in dancing, singing and rejoicing in the light.

Again did the Lord stretch forth his hands over Ethiopia and Canaan and the offsprings of Ham became mighty and the lands became prosperous in animals, fruits and grains. Great cities sprang up among them and the women as well as men mastered ships upon the waters.

And Athlyi looked and beheld great industries sprung up among the children of Ethiopia and he saw men kissing the women and praising them because of their mighty task in the struggle. He beheld women worshiping men because they had made them great.

And the Lord, our God, spoke unto the children, his voice echoed from Ethiopia to Canaan saying:

"Blessed are the mighty in righteousness for they shall

be respected." Blessed are the wealthy in love for I am rich and whosoever believeth in Athlyi and in the gospel which I have commended through him seeketh after these things which are in me."

"And I the Lord shall fill him to the brim and make his a power over which no hell shall prevail."

"But he that is contented in poverty and weakness shall be weaker and poorer, a foot stool of the nations; for he represents the devil, in him there is no God."

"The fool impoverishes himself to find me. Verily I say unto you, he shall not find me," saith the Lord, "for I am rich. But whosoever believeth in Athlyi seeketh my principle, therefore I shall reach out my hand and help him to be as I am."

CHAPTER 11

RETURNED TO NEWARK

And it came to pass that the word of the Lord, God of Ethiopia, came to Athlyi saying:

"Arise in the morning, break not your fast, neither say ye a word to anyone. And thou shall return to Newark and I will go with thee and thou shall see me."

"When thou shall have come to Newark prepare there a house, subsidiary to the House of Athlyi, where the children of Ethiopia shall assemble before me in united worship. I shall reach out my hands and bless them with increased blessings and they shall go forth as Athlyians with light and power, modeling all men according to my righteous principles," saith the Lord.

The Lord spake saying, "I will march with the Athlyians, I will pilot them, and stear them. I will recharge them and I, through their Shepherd, shall command them. Verily, there shall be no halting until they have conquered the Devil, banished His Hell and reconstruct the earth upon my righteous and clean principles."

"Then shall there be no prejudices, no illmosity among men, but peace tranquility and good will upon the earth, recognizing the divine fatherhood of God, the brotherhood of man and the rights of each and every one to enjoy equally the blessings of the Father."

And the Lord, God of Ethiopia, charged Athlyi saying, "Call not my Holy house 'Church' neither shall thou permit unjust literature which teaches that God has Commanded Israel to oppress, rob and destroy the offsprings of Ham in Canaan to rest upon my altar, for I have no part in such Deuteronomies. They are an abomination in my sight, and a disgrace upon the earth."

And the Lord continued, "I shall bring to an end the oppressors of Ham. I shall tear down the walls which I have Permitted to hold Ethiopia in bondage, that she may know the devil and his unrighteousness."

"Never-the-less, the children of Ethiopia, even unto this day, walketh upright before me, save those whom I the Lord God, have suffered to be spoiled by the enemies, that they might know the evil against the posterities of Ham."

"Now I shall send forth an army of Athlyians who shall redeem my children and deliver them again to my arms."

"I shall nourish them. Their chest shall be as

unbreakable steel. Their legs as giant reinforced concrete. Hearts of understanding and heads matchlessly wise. They shall be my masons, builders of a righteous kingdom and the source of salvation for all," saith the Lord. "For I am God, the creator of all. All things I hold in my hands and giveth freely unto him that walketh in me."

"Whosoever seeth an Athlyian, seeth me, for I am in him and he is of me. Whosoever followeth an Athlyian followeth me also," saith the Lord.

And when the Lord had spoke these things Athlyi turned and asked, "Father, what shall I call thy holy house?" And the Lord spoke to Athlyi saying, "Go and do as I have commanded you. The mouth of a child shall reveal the name; moreover, I shall write it upon the wall and you shall see it."

www.Wejees.net

CHAPTER 12

THE GUIDING LIGHT

Now when Athlyi started for Newark, there appeared a spotlight on the sleeve of his coat.

When Athlyi saw the light he tried to cover it with his hat but the light could not be covered.

Then he looked up and yelled joyfully, "It's the light of the Lord.

"Surely it cannot be covered. The light of the Lord our God I shall follow this day. Indeed I will not stray."

Athlyi journeyed to Newark and the light with him. But when he turned contrary to the will of God, the light would not follow but stood on another street.

Now when Athlyi saw the light would not go, he turned and went the way the light pointed him.

And it came to pass when Athlyi reached the City of Newark he prepared a house for the Lord our God and when he was making ready for the first sermon, a little girl opened the door and stared plumply into his face and uttered "Gaathly?" "Is your name Gaathly?" the shepherd asked. The child then raised her voice and again said "Gaathly," and went out.

Straightway a light flashed and Athlyi looked around. He beheld over the altar a hand, writing on the wall the name Gaathly.

When Athlyi saw the hand on the wall he became very fearful but embroiled with joy.

He then rushed into the inner chamber and proclaimed before his wife Miriam and his daughter Muriel, the name of Gaathly saying, "Behold a hand wrote it and the child revealed it as the Lord had promised."

From that day unto this the Holy House founded upon the Gospel of God through Athlyi is known as the Gaathly.

www.ChakraHealingSounds.com

CHAPTER 13

ATHLYI BLEEDS

And it came to pass on the third Saturday night of the seventh month of the year nineteen hundred and twenty-seven, the word of the Lord came to Athlyi saying, "Tomorrow, thou shalt with thine own blood set apart the Athlyians from the rest of the world's inhabitants, that I may glory in them and nourish them."

I shall send my angels and they shall dwell among the Athlyians and teach them new things. Verily, the women as well as the men shall develop great in science."

"Fear not, because of the inventions of today," saith the Lord, "for greater shall come out of my people, the Athlyians. They shall school Ethiopia. Consequently the sons and daughters of Ham shall be a burning light unto all the earth."

On the next day which was Sunday, while the Shepherd Athlyi preached before the people who came out to Gaathly, the spirit of the Lord came upon him and he then bit the top of his fingers, so that the blood spouted.

Then with his blood he marked a line between the Athlyians and the rest of the earth's inhabitants as the Lord had commanded him.

Then came forth the Shepherdmiss Muriel, daughter of Athlyi, who fell upon her knees saying, "Let thy blood fall upon me that I bear it through the ages." The shepherd let his blood fall upon her.

Then came forward also Sister Mary Howard, Stear of the Nourishers and Saints. She bound up the Shepherd's wound.

"I am a witness of this blood," the Stear uttered, but the Shepherd answered saying, "All Athlyians are witnesses of this blood, and I shall be their Shepherd forever. Even in the spirit I shall be with them and I shall be quick to answer those who called upon me in sincerity; but those who seeketh me empty in heart shall not find me.

"Happy shall be the aged who sacrifice the days of his youth within this blood. His tree shall grow mighty in the green pasture. He shall not want, but flourish."

"But verily I say unto you, only through concretation can anyone come beyond this blood and become an Athlyian.

"For unto the Athlyians, there is but one God, one Law, and one Shepherd."

"I am the lover of Justice, the light and guide unto perfect salvation saith Athlyi."

"Whosoever believeth in me shall in life enjoy salvation and inherit eternal happiness in the kingdom of God who sent me.

"But he that believeth not in me shall be a victim of slavery and oppression at the hands of Europe all the days of his unbelief.

"For he that receiveth me not, his heart despiseth the gift of God, the father, who sent me."

"For thus saith the Lord our God, I shall not send Japheth to Ham, neither will I send to Shem, Japheth. But in time of peril I shall appoint from among them a savior whose word shall reign forever."

"They that refuseth their own in me, shall find no

other. But slavery and oppression shall overcome them. They shall live in disgrace and die in dishonor."

"I am the almighty powerhouse," said the Lord, "the spring of salvation, but a people without a king has no connection with me."

"Fear not, O ye Athlyians, for I, Athlyi, am your Shepherd. I am not of the flesh but of the Spirit of God, the Father, who sent me to gather the children of Ethiopia that they be saved from peril. In the bosom of the Lord I shall forever hold my grip, therefore thou shalt be an everlasting light and power upon the earth."

CHAPTER 14

HEAVEN AND HELL

And it came to pass that the spirit moved in Athlyi and he became full with the holy ghost.

And he cried out saying, "Hear me O children of Ethiopia. There is not a heaven nor a hell but that which ye make of yourselves and for yourselves.

"In heaven there are few while in hell there are many. But those who are in heaven are the Champions of time who have conquered over sin and slothfulness."

"The fool slights the things in life and seeketh heaven after death.

"Verily, Verily I say unto you, he shall not find it. But the spirit of him that establishes a heaven on earth shall dwell in heaven everlasting.

"Unto him that is empty in love, faith, righteousness and industry there is no heaven."

"Heaven is a splendor. A source of peace and happiness where the spirit of God is visible in its appearance."

"He that passeth from this heaven is exalted into heaven eternal. Beyond strife and death, where pain and sorrows are unknown."

"Hell is a dark and shabby place; a den of thieves, murderers, gamblers, drunkards, liars, blasphemers, hypocrites, underminers, vooders, fortune tellers, begrudgers, raggedmen, yellers, backsliders, lazymen, deceivers, loafers, jormandizers, leppydoes, hoers, hoerlets, poverty, lice and diseases."

"Consequently the victims of the devil eat the fruit of the tree they have sown and therefore live in disgrace among men."

Woe be unto the spirit of him that passeth from this hell. He shall be lowered into eternal hell where peace and happiness are unknown.

He that is of the devil shall be segregated from the children of God; but he that is of God weareth the badge of the master, and the doors of heaven shall be opened unto him."

"Lo, I heard a cry in hell," saith Athlyi, "calling upon me in God. And I looked and beheld a man striving to conquer hell and escape from his horrible condition."

And Athlyi spoke unto him saying, "Who art thou?"

I am Amos who persecuted thee and lied about you. Now I would rather be a sweeper in the Gaathly than to be a prince in the palace of kings who believeth not in thee."

And Athlyi spoke unto him saying, "Thou doeth thyself this harm for there is no hell for him who believeth in me."

And Amos reached out crying, "Forgive me, O Athlyi and redeem me from this misery. For I believe that thou art a man of God with power to save."

Then Athlyi reached down and lifted him up saying, "Arise and stand above the devil and his hell. Thy faith in me shall bear thee up, but he that is weak in faith shall fall through his faith.

"For I am not of myself but of God, the Father, who is in me. He that gives himself up to me wholeheartedly, I shall nurse him at my breast and he shall be strong.

"There shall be no devil to conquer him, neither shall there be any hell to hold him; for they that are of me, shall help him that is in me. They that helpeth not their brother in me are not of me; likewise he who is not in harmony with the Law of this gospel is not of me.

"He that cometh unto me halfway, I shall not receive him," saith Athlyi, "for he is weak in himself in me and shall therefore fall in himself."

"He that withholds from me, that which he is able to

give, shall lose it without compensation; but he that soweth in me wholeheartedly shall reap a reward ten fold. For I am of good soil, and God p. 75 the Father in me, shall water that which is sown in me."

"In the lives of those that are in me," saith Athlyi, "there is but one God, one Shepherd, and one Gaathly. The Holy law is of God and is God with those in me."

"They that are of me shall help those that are in me. They shall march together to defend their dignity and create projects to supply their necessities in life.

"At the sound of the bugle of war all Athlyians shall gather around their Rulers. Then, at the Shepherd's command go forward to defend their rights.

"Knowing that our reward is Heaven everlasting if our enemy we shall conquer, it is therefore the sole spirit of the Athlyians to die in honor rather than to live as dependable dogs in disgrace, subject to the dictation of others who are not in me."

Then Athlyi called his Cledgers around him and placed his hands upon the right shoulder of each saying, "Blessed are the creators in me. They shall sit with me in heaven eternal and return with me to inspect the earth and crown the worthy.

"He that is not clean, industrious and thrifty is not in me, for I am a lover of cleanness, Lord of _{p. 76} industry and a builder of commerce, that men may be happy in me.

"For he that liveth a productive life in me, seeketh and shall obtain heaven terrestrial and heaven eternal.

"Go ye out upon the earth, beneath the earth, upon the waters, beneath the waters and upon the trees Gather in the blessings of God and develop them in me that ye prove yourself worthy of compensation. For weakness and poverty is of the devil but richness and power is of God.

"But where there is no love, righteousness, and faith in your transactions the glory of heaven shall vanish and the misery of hell shall occupy the soul."

www.SubliminalSelfHypnosis.com

CHAPTER 15

THE BEGGAR

And it came to pass that on the twenty-eighth day of the eighth month of nineteen hundred and twenty-seven (according to the English years but the fourteenth year according to the Athlican years) a young man twenty-two years of age came in to the Gaathly begging for money.

The shepherd looked upon the young man and said, "Thou art in the bloom of youth and power, but because thou art not of me, ye must beg.

"Go ye, however, through the highways and into comers, even so behind closed doors and gather men unto me, that they be lifted up from hell unto salvation.

"Then shall ye not be a beggar of me, but a sower and a reaper in me.

"For as many as believe and walk in me shall be saved. I shall relieve them of their miseries. I shall banish their sorrows. I shall defend them.

"I shall be a light in their darkness. I shall raise them up when all hopes are dead.

I shall harden my heart against backsliders, the hypocrite, the liar, and the thief, I despise.

"Be aware of the gospels that are not of God through Ethiopia. For it shall rob and destroy as many as accept it.

"Verily I say unto you, he that is not of me is not for your salvation. For I am he whom the Lord, God of Ethiopia, had promised thee from creation, that ye may stretch forth thy hands direct unto the Father through me and be saved.

"Before me there was none unto Ethiopia, but with me there is another and you, in me, in him are one with God; and the offspring of my vein and the offspring of his vein are cousins.

"Take heed! O ye children of Ethiopia. For I Athlyi zigy sobcok tee. Whosoever cometh after me and is not of me is not for your salvation, but seeketh to destroy your civilization in God through me.

"Prophets shall rise and wise men shall spring out of

you, but they that build not upon this foundation in me, in righteousness are deceivers of you.

"They shall come up to you with unjust gospels, which seeketh to destroy the offsprings of our father, Ham, doctrines which were before me.

"But it shall be as a man pleading with an electrician to go back to the tallow candle age, but the electrician shall laugh him to scorn.

"For I am greater than all gospels that were before my coming. I am richer. I am higher. Test me and be ye convinced that I, in the bosom of the God of Justice, have laid a foundation sufficient to hold all the builders that cometh after me in righteousness.

I shall banish the devil. I shall clear up his hell and it shall bloom like a garden of brimigen. Then shall the rivers of peace flow out and the children of all the earth shall sit around the table of salvation in the house of God enjoying life the splendor of true love and justice in me. For I am not myself, but God in me unto you.

"But verily I say unto you, I shall cut my heaven from him that knoweth and doeth not according the gospel.

"The wise will prepare for battle even though there may not be any fight.

"The fool will quarrel but he that quarrels with a fool is a damn fool. Hear me, oh thou Athlyians! Be ye wise and live I go to prepare a place for you beyond this heaven.

"Whosoever walketh in my blood within the principles of this gospel shall dwell with me in p. 80 heaven everlasting, but he that walketh another way shall not find me."

"I will blow my trumpet throughout the kingdom of Athlyi in Africa," saith the lord our God, "and my people the Athlyians shall blow it unto the world.

"Then shall the inhabitants of the earth respect me, for I am a God of salvation, a conqueror of evil."

And it came to pass that Athlyi issued an order saying," A real minister of Athlicanity must bear a diploma from the Athlican School of Athlicology and the graduation process shall embody ordination.

"God be with you my beloved. Let there be unity in

spirit while ye are absent one from another. Wheresoever it is one Athlyian there is the shepherd in him, and whatsoever heareth an Athlyian, heareth also the Shepherd, and whatsoever an Athlyian seeth, seeth the Shepherd also, for the Athlyians are an amalgation instituted by God which no man can separate."

For deeply healing and transformational self hypnosis, subliminal and sound healing programs on MP3, MP4, CD and DVD, plus free downloads, visit:
www.SubliminalSelfHypnosis.com

THE THIRD BOOK OF ATHLYI NAMED THE FACTS OF THE APOSTLES

CHAPTER 1

APOSTLES ANOINTED

Just at the time when the nations of the earth through their ill education and oppression, believeth that they had ruined the children of Ethiopia for ever, and that they would be satisfied with the crumbs of life.

Behold the great Almighty hath commanded his angels to anoint them that they be a new and prolific people upon the earth.

Then did the lord God with his own hands ordain three apostles and sent them forth to save Ethiopia's generation from doom.

Now when Marcus Garvey, God's foremost apostle,

heard the voice of his colleague, apostle Robert Lincoln Poston, preaching in the city of Detroit, Michigan, United States of America, he knew that this was his colleague for the lord God hath revealed, notwithstanding the three apostles had met in the spirit before they came to administer the law Gospel for the full salvation of Ethiopia's posterities.

And it came to pass the apostle Garvey journeyed to Detroit and there met his colleagues and they greeted each other with great joy, and the heart of was the heart of other.

Now when the amalgamation of their apostleship was verified, apostle Poston came to New York City, United States of America, and then teamed with apostle Garvey in the work for the redemption of Ethiopia and her trodden posterities, whom through the oppression of the nations and the ignorance of the Negro ministers of Christian faith, were hanging over the bridge of death, both body and soul.

CHAPTER 2

GOD SPOKE TO HIS APOSTLES

Now in the year nineteen hundred and twenty-three, the word of the Lord God of Ethiopia came to apostle Marcus Garvey saying, where is thy colleague?

And he answered, "Father, behold he is with me."

"Call together the children of Ethiopia, saith the Lord, that they may know my request, and send forth a mission unto the land of Ethiopia which I hath given to her children from the beginning of the world, that they prepare a foundation for all the posterities of Ethiopia, even unto the end.

"For I, the Lord God, shall come to judge between the three races of men; woe be unto the empty handed, the slothful and the coward. I shall bring judgement upon them with fire and with brimstone, even the baby at the mother's breast shall not escape," saith the Lord. "Prepare ye a bill of arrangement," saith the Lord, "and give it in the hands of thy colleague that he go to the land of Ethiopia (Africa) and to the nations at the entrance of the land and request then to open the door for the return of thy children.

"And I, the Lord, shall go with him, and I will touch the hearts of the nations and they shall yield to the request.

"Then shall the children of Ethiopia return to their own land and there establish a light with no nation shall compare, nor will there be any power sufficient to douse it.

"For I am the Lord God of Ethiopia and I shall dwell with mine a anointed and they shall be my people as long as they follow the teachings of my apostles.

"Moreover, behold at thy side is the noble woman Henrietta in whom the whole heaven adore because of her greatness of faith and the loyal way in which she fights to save Ethiopia and her generations from everlasting downfall. Place her at the side of thy colleague, for great is her wisdom, saith the Lord, and send ye also another t at they go and prepare a home for mine anointed."

And it came to pass that apostle Garvey obeyed the Lord, and he called the children of Ethiopia and there gathered a great host in the City of New York.

And when the apostle put before them the Lord's request they leapt for joy and confirmed the will of the Lord God of Ethiopia.

Then were a delegation of three sent forth according to the words of the Lord.

CHAPTER 3

STANDING BEFORE ELIJAH

And it came to pass on the night of the fifteenth day of the third month of the nineteen hundred and twenty-fourth year, Athlyi spake aloud, saying:

"Behold I saw the heaven draped in black, and I saw Angel Douglas sitting in a mourning robe, moreover the celestial saints of Ethiopia were deep in sorrow.

"And it came to pass that I continued to look, and behold I saw a natural man standing before Angel Douglas, and after a brief conversation, the mighty Angel conveyed him to the throne Elijah, God of heaven and the earth.

"Then upon the head the natural man did Elijah place a crown on the front part of the crown there was a brilliant star whose light extended from heaven to the earth.

"Now when the crown was bestowed upon him, behold the mourning apparel disappeared and there was joy in heaven.

And it came to pass that I saw a great host of Negroes marching upon the earth and there was a light upon them, then I looked towards the heaven and behold I saw the natural man standing in the east and the star of his crown gave light to the pathway of the children of Ethiopia."

CHAPTER 4

APOSTLES EXALTED

The following morning after Athlyi's vision, Athlyi looked towards the rising sun and cried out saying, "My God, My God, what shall happen to the apostles of the Twentieth Century? Father if it's me, even I that shall pass from the presence of men grant that the Piby live forever that the children of Ethiopia, through the teaching of the Afro Athlican Constructive Church, may obtain salvation forever."

And it came to pass that the Lord spake to Athlyi saying: "In the flesh did he go prepare a foundation for the generation of Ethiopia, But in the spirit will he return to lead them there upon.

"For I, the Lord, hath exalted him in the spirit, Prince over the children of Ethiopia; he shall see with all seeing eyes, in vain shall the nations of the world lay traps before mine anointed, for the prince of the children shall lead them.

"Woe be unto the proud, the hard hearted, unto those who shall say I have my treasures here I will not leave them, neither will I follow the host led by the apostles of the twentieth century."

"I shall bring vengeance upon them," saith the lord, "they be better boiled in oil, for I shall have no mercy upon them."

THE FOURTH BOOK OF ATHLYI CALLED PRECAUTION

CHAPTER I

A BUGGY FROM TOKIO TO LOS ANGELES, A BICYCLE FROM LONDON TO ANGUILLA

Now in the fifteenth year of Athlyi's reign over Athlyians, the spirit of the Lord came upon him.

Being filled with the Holy Ghost he prophesied saying, "To the sun, in the sun, with the sun and the fuel of today shall a used to be."

How beautiful the ships. How powerful, but the fuel today shall a used to be. How speedy the air-ships the world around, around and around with no need for refuel.

Hot shall be the houses. The pots a-boiling and bright the lights; but where are the wire? They used to be.

"The power of today is electric, but tomorrow shall be siprick. Satter, the mighty comet shall pass with the end of her tail two miles from the earth and the roaring of her passing, killing."

"I heard a cry saying, 'Where is thy scenery as a star O Scatter. Behold thou art lands over lands. Pass quickly for we perish beneath thee."

"New lands when Satter came back. A buggy from Tokio to Los Angeles. A bicycle from London to Anguilla.

"The Atlantic and Pacific shall prepare to receive their wilderness and it shall be seen them adorning as a bride to receive her groom.

"New animals, new furs, a strange people and the winter of today shall a used to be.

"The ice in the north and the ice in the south shall disappear. Then shall continents which are submerged arise and the whole earth shall bloom.

"O sun, thou outlet of the inter-planetical fumes, shine on. For with thee, he shall sit in his parlor in Athlyi, Africa, and see his daughter flirting in Chicago, U.S.A.

"He shall rebuke her with his mouth and she shall hear him, then reply with the wave of her hand and he rebuke her with his mouth and she shall hear him, then reply with the wave of her hand and he shall see her.

"In his parlor he shall see a rooster treading in the moon and the bees on the roses in Venus.

"The laborers in Mars, strike-breakers on earth and my daughter in college in Jupiter.

"How hard it is when ye know not how, but he that is in me shall know that mysteries of mysteries which are hidden from him in these days.

"But I shall feed him with my own hands so that he takes one bite at a time and one swallow at a time else ye be choked.

"My boys shall remind you of the things I have

forgotten, for I have seen so far, but those that cometh after me, of me, with me and upon our God shall see farther even than I."

"Verily, Verily, I am the seed," saith Athlyi "but the Lord, God of Ethiopia, is the sower, and ye are the trees of me that shall bring forth fruit a million fold.

"But he that beareth not is he that has not me in his heart and shall therefore receive no reward of me.

"I have not reached the height but they that are of me shall extend me. I have, however, dug deep and laid the foundation of eternal salvation. I have made thick the walls, I have sunk deeper the center pillars and lined them with steel. The reinforcements I have made of steel for I am conscious of the height that shall be attained on me. A development beyond words.

"I am black. Made in the image and likeness of the God of our Fathers and is of the Lord, our God unto thee.

"He that established himself in me is with God and welleth upon an efficient foundation, but he that buildeth not on me establishes himself on nothing of consequence for the children of Ham."

"La Alpha Elijah cr toco coruse, ninky mose zezom la jobijem."

CHAPTER 2

HELD OUT HIS MORSEL

And it came to pass that Athlyi sat in the sanctuary of the House of Athlyi with his left hand under his chin and the morsel in his right hand, apparently he was present in person but in the spirit he was not.

His mind went afar and entered the characteristic of the human tie. Suddenly he stretched forth his morsel and uttered saying, "Sons of Athlyi, arise! Lift your heads and take heed. Let the sublimity of my words reign in your hearts and in the hearts of your offsprings forever.

"Verily, Verily, I say unto you, poverty is of the devil but it is better that ye choose to be poor than to live in the richness of the richest with a woman whose heart is contrary to thine.

"The deeds of a contrary couple are destructive and their destiny is Hell everlasting.

I plead a divorce, my beloved, because I leadeth thee south but thou goeth north. I point east but thy desire is west. Depart therefore that ye find a man who seeth and goeth in thy own direction that it be well with thee; for a tug-o-war in the mind of horror to the soul. Moreover the treasury of the richest is not sufficient to supply the consumption of the contrary spirit.

"For a man no height is two high to achieve in me. No obstacle is too great for him to remove when conscious that this woman is with him indeed. Blessed is the household where the couple can map out the future with patience, peace and understanding, but a quarrelsome woman is a road to hell. Let so be said even of the man."

And Athlyi reached out the morsel again and said, "Hear ye, O daughters of Athlyi! Verily I say unto you, the hopes and salvation of a woman is in the man, whose trust is in the Lord, our God, in me.

"But he that is not in me is far from God and has

nothing of consequence for a brag.

"For I am the rock, the spring and power grounded in God. Dwell in me, with love and righteousness in faith, patience, cleanness and constructiveness. My spirit in thee shall never die.

"Verily I say unto all nations, the Athlyians are not too proud to sacrifice whatever is necessary to obtain justice and to establish peace on earth, for when righteousness is lacking there is no tranquility.

"Our motto is peace. Our standard is Right. Our hopes are salvation."

CHAPTER 3

THE CLEAN SHOULD NOT ACCEPT THE INVITATIONS OF THE UNCLEAN

The spirit of the Lord moved within Athlyi. Being full with the Holy Ghost the Shepherd spake saying:

"Thou giveth the fat of thy life to the devil. Now that thou art drained and can no longer stand, ye cometh to God with your bones." "But I shall not accept them," saith the Lord, "for I am God who giveth thee to eat and to drink. I am he who supplies the necessities of life. Shall my reward be that ye dump your garbage on me."

"Unto him whom thou giveth the fat of thy life dump also thy bones, that ye bear in fullness the consequence of you wickedness, for the body of the wicked shall be cast into the grave and his soul in hell eternal. For the spirit of the body that abideth in earthly hell shall be a prisoner in hell everlasting."

And the word of the Lord came to Athlyi saying, "He that giveth unto me that fat of his life by his usefulness for the welfare of the living, When I the lord shall transform him from the earth, I shall exalt him into heaven everlasting where he shall live forever with me in peace and splendor."

"Whosoever I forgive shall rise to serve me, but whosoever I have not forgiven shall not rise."

"He that passeth away in me shall dwell with my saints in glory," saith the Lord. "But the spirit of the body of him that passeth away in the devil shall not enter my fold, but shall dwell in everlasting torment."

And Athlyi spake saying, "Life without pleasure within capacity is displeasing to God, but, in your amusements dance ye mild else ye offend the Master."

"The clean should not accept the invitations of the unclean to gossip with them for the Lord abideth in the clean in spirit."

CHAPTER 4

SHALL SUFFER

And it came to pass that Athlyi spake saying I shall be dragged about, mocked, scorned, and prosecuted because of this gospel, which the Lord, God of Ethiopia, has commanded unto you through me. Many of you who follow me this day will desert your shepherd because of fear. But blessed are the brave and faithful. They shall be ruler over rulers.

"Thine enemy shall shed your blood because of this Holy Piby, but the blood of thy veins shall richen the soil for the gospel. I am Messiah unto Ethiopia, therefore my word reign forever and ever.

I shall be cast into prison for your sake, but my spirit shall go out of jail and fight for Ethiopia.

"Nations shall perish because of my persecution, for I am not a mere man but a Messiah upon the earth. Whosoever persecuteth me, committeth a crime against the Holy Ghost, in which there is no forgiveness, therefore the consequence is hell eternal.

"The Athlyians, God's selected people, who are of never dying faith and perseverance shall p. 99 increase in power. Their women shall breed like rabbits and the Green Pasture shall aid in their protection. Verily the Athlyians shall be numberless upon the earth and the spirit of the Lord shall guide them."

And Athlyi spake saying, "It shall come to pass that the devil will make hollow ground in the pathway of the Athlyians, but they shall march upon him with the Holy Piby and he shall step back and fall into his own ditch.

"Verily I say unto you, if a hay stack can stop a blazing fire then shall the workers of the devil impede the advancing Athlyians whose development has no boundary but the mocker shall perish.

"Thou despiseth me when I was weak, now that I am strong, ye come? Verily, Verily, neither my milk nor my cream shall be for thee, but shall be for those who supported me in my tender age.

"Yea, it shall be said Athlyi, in spite of all obstacles, he climbed with the burdens of Ham, and when he reached the top, the Heaven and Earth shouted, Behold! He has conquered, and an angel of the Lord decended and crowned him."

La jobijem dilt ze larky, inty met. Zeth Athlyi.

And Athlyi spake saying, "Forgive twice but in the offence thou shalt not forgive."

QUESTIONS

AND ANSWERS

Questions and answers concerning the works of God among the children of Ethiopia and the principles of Athlicanity.

Q1. What is the house of Athlyi?

A. A house created by the Almighty God through his apostle Athlyi, giver of the Gospel and the law commanded by the Lord of the salvation of Ethiopia's posterities.

Q2. What is the right wing to the house of Athlyi?

A. The Afro Athlican Constructive Church.

Q3. What is the left wing to the house of Athlyi?

A. The Athlican green pasture.

Q4. Can there be any other church or denomination save the Afro Athlican constructive church upon the law or the Gospel commanded by God to save the generations of Ethiopia?

A. No.

Q5. What is Athlicanity?

A. The Law and the Gospel administered by Athlyi.

Q6. Why can no other church be established upon this gospel?

A. Because the Athlicanity is sent by the Lord our God not to teach confusion and hatred but to set up a real religious and material brotherhood among the children of Ethiopia.

Q7. What is the Holy Piby?

A. Holy book of God written unto the generations of Ethiopia.

Q8. Do the Athlyians believe in Jesus Christ?

A. As a true servant sent by God to seek and to save the lost house of Israel.

Q9. Who did Athlyi, Marcus Garvey and colleagues come to save?

A. The down trodden children of Ethiopia that they may raise to be a great power among the nations and the glory of their God.

Q10. What is the Dictuary?

A. The most holy place in the Afro Athlican Constructive Church or in the house of p.102 Athlyi, where the Shepherd or his apostles occupies to administer the gospel.

Q11. What is God's Holy law to the children of Ethiopia?

A. A written document handed to Athlyi by an angel of the Lord whose name was Douglas.

Q12. What is the difference between God's holy law to the children of Israel and God's Holy Law to the children of Ethiopia?

A. There is much difference, the holy law to the Israelites was given to Moses, but God's Holy Law given to the children of Ethiopia was handed to Athlyi by a messenger of the Lord our God, notwithstanding in the law given to the Israelites there are ten commandments, but in the law given to the children of Ethiopia there are twelve.

Q13. What church is already established on God's Holy Law given to the children of Ethiopia?

A. The Afro Athlican Constructive Church.

Q14. By what other name shall this church be known?

A. The house of Athlyi.

THE SHEPHERD'S COMMAND BY ATHLYI

First: Let all literature for the instruction of Athlyian's children be of a constructive nature looking towards Ethiopia.

Second: Let the eye of a star be the eye of the Shepherd and the ear of a star be the ear of the Shepherd, for they are his stars.

Third: Fight for that which is yours and ye shall obtain it, for there is nothing hard against the power of God.

Printed in Great Britain
by Amazon